Girl Empowered! Confident & Connected

A Teen Girl's Guide to Social Skills, Handling Rejection, and Real Friendships

Victoria Penley

Creative Scribbles, LLC

Disclaimer

This book is intended for educational and informational purposes only. It is not intended to diagnose, treat, cure, or prevent any mental health condition, nor should it be considered a substitute for professional medical, psychological, counseling, or educational advice.

The author shares general information, strategies, and encouragement based on research, experience, and personal perspectives. Every individual and situation is unique, and readers should seek guidance from a qualified professional regarding specific concerns related to mental health, emotional well-being, relationships, or personal circumstances.

Parents, guardians, teachers, and caregivers are encouraged to use their own judgment when discussing the topics presented in this book with teens.

The author and publisher assume no responsibility for any actions taken based on the information contained in this book.

ALSO BY VICTORIA PENLEY

The Oddly Comforting Books Collection

Delightfully Unnecessary. Surprisingly Meaningful.

Thoughtful humor, observations, and emotional support disguised as sarcasm. Books that somehow make ordinary things feel deeply important.

Thank You for Being a Lamp
A Surprisingly Heartfelt Reflection on Overlooked Things, Quiet Usefulness, and Ordinary Importance

Wait, Is This How You've Been Living?
A Story of Misplaced Souls, Refrigerator Raids, and the Truth About the Backyard

The Parking Lot Has Won Again
A Deeply Unqualified Study of Human Attention Span

The Girl Empowered! Series

Practical, encouraging guides designed to help teen girls build confidence, healthy relationships, emotional resilience, and a strong sense of self.

Each book in the Girl Empowered! series can be read as a standalone guide and purchased separately. While the books complement one another, there is no required reading order. Start with the topic that matters most to you right now.

Girl Empowered!
A Two-In- One Guide and Workbook for Confidence, Friendship, and Social Anxiety in Today's Digital World

Confident & Connected
A Teen Girl's Guide to Social Skills, Handling Rejection, and Real Friendships

Strong & Unstoppable
A Teen Girl's Guide to Boundaries, Assertiveness, and Using Your Voice

Smart & Secure
A Teen Girl's Guide to Trusting Yourself, Recognizing Red Flags, and Making Wise Decisions

Worthy & Enough
A Teen Girl's Guide to Self-Worth, Confidence, and Positive Body Image

Purpose & Possibility

A Teen Girl's Guide to Discovering Your Strengths, Pursuing Your Purpose, and Building a Meaningful Future

Dating Smart

A Teen Girl's Guide to Healthy Relationships, Red Flags, Boundaries, and Self-Respect

CONTENTS

Introduction

Friendships can be amazing, exciting, comforting, confusing, awkward, emotional, and exhausting, sometimes all in the same week. During the teen years, social situations can start to feel bigger than they really are. One awkward conversation can replay in your mind for hours. One unanswered text can suddenly make you question everything. Feeling left out, misunderstood, embarrassed, or rejected can hurt deeply, especially when it feels like everyone else has friendship figured out except you.

This book was written to remind you of something important: you are not the only one who feels this way. Social confidence is not something people are simply born with. It is a skill that grows over time through experience, self-awareness, and learning how to handle uncomfortable moments without letting them define you. Inside these pages, you will learn practical ways to navigate friendships, conversations, rejection, social anxiety, and the pressure to fit in—while becoming more confident in who you already are.

WHY SOCIAL SITUATIONS FEEL BIGGER THAN THEY ARE

LILY TOLD HERSELF SHE would try talking to someone new today.

After the fourth period, she saw a group of girls from her science class laughing near the lockers. She recognized two of them. She'd talked to one about homework once. *Just go over there,* she thought. *It's not a big deal.* She walked up and said, "Hey, what are you guys talking about?"

One girl glanced at her. "Oh, just this video," she said, turning her phone back toward the group.

The conversation kept moving. Lily stood there for a second. Not long. Maybe three seconds. But it felt much longer. No one was rude. No one told her to leave. But no one pulled her in either. Her brain reacted instantly. *That was awkward. They don't want me here. Why did I even try? I should've just stayed quiet.* By the time she walked away, her mind had already turned one slightly uncomfortable moment into a full social disaster.

If something like this has ever happened to you, pause for a second. You are not weird. You are not socially doomed. And you are not the only one whose brain goes into dramatic overreaction mode. Social situations can feel much bigger than they actually are. Let's talk about why.

Your Brain Hates Uncertainty

Your brain does not like moments of uncertainty. When something feels unfinished, like a group not immediately including you, your brain quickly creates a story to explain it. And unfortunately, that story usually isn't flattering.

"They don't like me." "I embarrassed myself." "I should've never tried."

But here's the truth: Most of the time, you don't have enough information to know that. Maybe they were already deep into a conversation. Maybe they didn't process fast enough to shift. Maybe they assumed you'd jump in naturally. Maybe they were awkward, too. Your brain doesn't pause to consider those possibilities first. It jumps to: *Something is wrong with me.* That jump is automatic. It does not mean it's accurate.

The Spotlight Effect (In Real Life)

Have you ever noticed how intensely aware you are of your own awkward moments? You remember how long you stood there. You remember the tone of someone's voice. You remember exactly how your stomach dropped. But most people are usually just as focused on themselves.

There's something called the "spotlight effect." It simply means we assume everyone is watching and judging us, when in reality, most people are thinking about their own words, their own hair, their own next sentence. That girl who said, "Oh, just this video"? She was probably thinking about the video. Not about you. But your brain, trying to protect you, decided the moment was huge. It probably wasn't.

Awkward Is Not the Same as Rejection

This is an important distinction. Awkward means a moment didn't flow smoothly. Rejection means someone clearly and intentionally pushed you away. Those are not the same thing. Sometimes a group doesn't instantly open up because they're distracted, they don't shift conversations easily, they assume you'll join naturally, or they didn't realize you felt unsure. An awkward pause is not the same as being rejected. But when you care about belonging, it can feel that way. And feelings can be loud, even when they're not fully accurate.

Separate the Event from the Story

Here's a simple reset tool you can use anytime something feels socially uncomfortable. Separate the event from the story. The event is what happened. The story is what your brain told you about it.

For Lily, the event was:

• She walked over. • She asked a question. • Someone answered. • The conversation continued.

That's it.

The story was:

"They don't like me." "I embarrassed myself." "I shouldn't have tried."

Stories feel real. But they are interpretations, not facts. And interpretations can be very wrong.

A Steadier Way to Read the Moment

Instead of jumping to the worst conclusion, try this steadier interpretation: "They were already mid-conversation. It didn't flow. That happens sometimes. I can try again another time." That's not pretending everything went perfectly. It's choosing balance over panic. Social confidence isn't about eliminating awkward moments. It's about not turning every awkward moment into a personal failure.

What to Do Next (The Micro-Recovery Plan)

If you decide the moment was just awkward, not rejection, here's your next step. Don't overanalyze it for hours. Give it space. Then, within a day or two, try again in a low-pressure way.

That might look like:

• A short comment in class • A quick response in a group chat • Laughing at something small • Asking one simple follow-up question

You don't need a big entrance. You need consistency. Confidence grows from repeated small attempts, not from a single perfect moment.

Try Something New This Week: Challenge your Assumptions.

The next time something feels socially uncomfortable, pause before replaying it repeatedly. Ask yourself, was I rejected, or was it just awkward? Then remind yourself that awkward is survivable. And trying again is powerful. Social confidence isn't built in perfect conversations. It's built in imperfect ones, the kind where you show up, feel unsure, and try anyway. And you already did that.

When Conversations Fall Flat and How to Recover

MAYA DECIDED SHE WAS going to be brave.

In English class, the teacher had just assigned a group project. Maya ended up next to two girls she didn't know very well. When the class broke into groups, she tried first. "So... what topic do you guys want to pick?" she asked.

One girl shrugged. "I don't know."

The other said, "Whatever."

Silence. Maya felt it immediately, that heavy, uncomfortable pause that stretches just a little too long. Her mind raced.

Say something else. No, that was weird. Why is this so hard?

She laughed a little, the nervous kind, and then stopped talking. The conversation picked up again a minute later, but Maya had already decided the moment had gone badly. If you've ever felt a conversation fall flat like that, you know how uncomfortable it can be. But here's something important. A flat moment does not mean you failed. It means you're human.

Conversations Don't Always Flow

We sometimes imagine that socially confident people move smoothly through every interaction. They don't. Conversations stall. People give short answers. Someone says something that doesn't quite land. That doesn't mean the connection is ruined. It means conversations are built in real time, and real time can be messy. The problem isn't the silence. The problem is what your brain does during the silence.

The "This Is Going Badly" Spiral

When a conversation slows down, your brain often jumps in with commentary. That commentary feels urgent and convincing.

They're bored. I'm not interesting. I should stop talking.

But remember what we talked about in the last chapter. Your brain hates uncertainty. Silence feels uncertain, and your brain fills it with a story. But a pause is not proof of failure. Sometimes it's just... a pause.

What to Do When There's Silence

Instead of panicking, try one of these simple resets:

Option 1: Expand the Question

If someone answers, “I don’t know,” you can respond with: “Would you rather do something easier or something more creative?”

Now you’ve given them structure.

Option 2: Share First

If no one is offering ideas, try: “I was thinking we could do the social media topic. That one seemed interesting.”

Sometimes people are quiet because they’re unsure. Offering something concrete gives the conversation direction.

Option 3: Light Acknowledgment

If the silence feels obvious, you can even say gently, “We’re all thinking hard, huh?” Said with a small smile, which can instantly reset tension. Silence isn’t dangerous. It just feels louder than it is.

When Your Words Don’t Land

Sometimes you say something and... it just doesn’t get much response. You make a joke. No one laughs. You share a story. Someone changes the subject. That stings. But before deciding it was a disaster, consider a few calmer possibilities.

• They didn’t hear you clearly. • They were distracted. • They process humor differently. • They were already thinking about what to say next.

Not every flat reaction is rejection. Sometimes it’s just mismatched timing. Even very socially confident people sometimes say things that don’t land. They don’t treat it like a personal crisis.

The Three-Second Recovery Rule

Here's a simple tool you can use when something feels awkward mid-conversation. Give it three seconds. Instead of filling the space with nervous over-talking, take a breath. Let the moment settle. Then either:

• Ask a follow-up question • Offer a new idea • Or calmly let someone else speak

You don't have to rescue every pause. Sometimes confidence looks like staying steady.

What Not to Do

When a conversation feels awkward, your brain may want to:

• Stop talking entirely • Leave abruptly • Overexplain • Apologize for nothing • Replay it all day

None of those helps. Instead, aim for neutral recovery. Neutral recovery sounds like: "That didn't flow perfectly. That's okay." Then you continue. No dramatic exit required.

Confidence Is Built in Micro-Moments

Here's something most teens don't realize. Social confidence isn't built in the big, impressive moments. It's built in small recoveries. The time you asked one more question. The time you stayed instead of walking away. The time you tried again. That's growth. Not perfection.

Try Something New This Week.

This week, if a conversation feels awkward: Notice the pause. Don't panic. Use one follow-up question or offer one idea. That's it. No overthinking. No dramatic conclusions. Just one steady response. Because conversations don't have to be perfect to move forward, they have to keep moving. And so do you.

What to Do When Someone Doesn't Respond the Way You Expected

Ava stared at her phone. She had finally worked up the courage to text a girl from her soccer team.

"Hey! Are you going to the game on Friday?"

Three minutes passed. Then ten. Then an hour.

Finally, a reply popped up: "Maybe."

That was it. No emoji. No follow-up question. No excitement. Ava's stomach dropped.

Maybe? What does that mean? She doesn't want to talk to me. Why did I even text her?

Within seconds, Ava's brain had written a full story about that one-word reply. If you've ever felt your mood shift because of a short response, a flat tone, or a quiet reaction, you're not alone. But here's something important. Short responses are not always personal. Even when they feel personal.

The Expectation Gap

When you start a conversation, you usually have an expectation in your head.

You imagine:

They'll respond with enthusiasm. They'll ask something back. They'll match your energy.

When their response doesn't match what you pictured, it feels disappointing. Sometimes it even feels like rejection. But there's a difference between "They didn't match my expectations" and "They rejected me." Those are not the same thing.

Why Responses Can Feel Flat

There are dozens of reasons someone might respond briefly or without much emotion:

• They're distracted. • They're tired. • They're multitasking. • They're not big texters. • They don't use emojis. • They're unsure how to respond.

None of those automatically means: "I don't like you."

But your brain may jump there first. Because uncertainty feels uncomfortable. And your brain would rather assume the worst than sit in uncertainty.

Don't Mind-Read

When someone responds in a way you didn't expect, your mind may try to fill in invisible details.

"She sounds annoyed." "She's bored." "She doesn't want me around."

But unless someone clearly says something unkind, you don't know what they're thinking. Mind-reading is one of the fastest ways to damage your own confidence.

Instead of mind-reading, try this: Stick to what you do know. Ava knows: She sent a text. The girl replied. The reply was short. That's it. Everything else is interpretation.

How to Respond Without Spiraling

If you get a short reply like "Maybe," you have options.

You can gently continue: "Oh, cool! Let me know, it should be fun."

Or: "I might go too. I'm trying to decide."

This keeps the tone neutral and confident. You're not chasing. You're not apologizing. You're simply continuing. And if the other person doesn't engage further? That's information. Not judgment.

When It Happens In Person

Sometimes it's not a text. It's a shrug. A distracted "Yeah." Or someone is checking their phone while you're talking. That can sting. Before assuming the worst, pause and ask yourself: Is this about me, or is this about them? Sometimes people are socially tired, having a bad day, nervous, or just not expressive. A flat response doesn't automatically mean you did something wrong.

The Confidence Reset

When someone doesn't respond the way you expected, try this reset:

Pause. Separate the event from the story. Choose a steady follow-up or let it go calmly. Confidence isn't about getting the perfect response every time. It's about staying steady when you don't.

What If It Actually Is Disinterest?

Let's be honest. Sometimes someone isn't that interested in building a friendship. That doesn't mean you're unworthy. It means: Not everyone connects deeply with everyone. Compatibility matters. Shared interests matter. Energy match matters. When someone doesn't respond warmly, that's not proof you failed. It may simply mean you're not a close match, and that's okay. You are not required to be everyone's person.

Try Something New This Week

The next time someone gives a short or flat response:

Don't immediately lower your confidence. Respond once in a steady way. If they engage, great. If they don't, you've learned something useful. Not about your worth. About your fit. Social confidence grows when you stop measuring your value by other people's tone. And that's something you can practice every single day.

When You Feel Left Out

Sofia learned about the party on Instagram. She wasn't invited. She didn't even know it was happening until she saw the photos, a group of girls from school smiling in someone's living room, holding red plastic cups filled with soda, laughing like they'd been planning it for weeks. Sofia stared at the pictures longer than she meant to.

Why didn't they invite me? Did I do something? Do they even like me? Was everyone invited except me?

Her chest felt tight. Not angry exactly. Not even surprised. Just... small. If you've ever found out about something you weren't included in, you know that feeling. It's not loud like embarrassment. It's quieter. But it can hurt more.

Being Left Out Hits Deep

Here's something important to understand. Belonging matters. Humans are wired for connection. When we feel excluded, even in small ways, our brains react strongly. That doesn't make you dramatic. It makes you human. The problem isn't that it hurts. The problem is the story your brain may attach to the hurt.

The Stories We Tell Ourselves

When you feel left out, your mind may jump to conclusions like:

"They don't like me." "I'm not important." "I'm always the extra friend." "I'll never fit in."

Those thoughts feel true in the moment. But they are interpretations, not confirmed facts. Let's slow it down. What are the actual possibilities?

• It was a smaller gathering. • They invited people they sit with every day. • Someone else organized it. • It wasn't meant to exclude you personally. • They assumed you were busy.

Are all of those guaranteed? No. But neither is the worst-case version. When something hurts, your brain looks for a clear explanation. It often chooses the harshest one.

Not Every Invitation Is a Measure of Your Worth

This is a difficult but freeing truth. You will not be included in everything. No one is. Even socially confident girls experience moments of exclusion. The difference is how they interpret it.

Instead of deciding, "I wasn't invited because I'm not good enough."

They think: "That event happened. I wasn't part of it. That doesn't define me."

That's steadiness.

Group Dynamics Are Complicated

Friend groups are rarely as simple as they look in photos.

There are:

• Sub-groups within groups • People who are closer to some than others • Situations that grow out of shared classes or activities • Plans made quickly without deep thought

Sometimes you're not included because of proximity, not because you're rejected. It doesn't mean you don't matter. It means social circles are fluid. And fluid doesn't mean permanent.

What Not to Do When You Feel Left Out

When exclusion stings, your brain may suggest:

• Posting something to make them notice you • Sending a dramatic text • Pulling away completely • Deciding you'll never try again

Those reactions feel powerful in the moment. But they rarely create the outcome you want. Instead, aim for calm. Not pretending it doesn't hurt. Just not letting the hurt control your next move.

A Steady Response

If you find out about something you weren't invited to, try this:

Feel it, without judging yourself for feeling it. Separate the event from the story. Stay consistent in your normal interactions. You don't need to act colder. You don't need to overcompensate. You don't need to prove anything. Steady confidence often looks quiet.

When It Keeps Happening

If you consistently feel left out around the same group, that's information. Not about your worth. It's about compatibility within that group.

Sometimes the healthiest move isn't forcing your way into a circle. It's expanding your circle.

That might mean talking more with someone in a different class, joining a new club or activity, or strengthening one-on-one friendships. Belonging grows where effort is mutual. You don't have to chase it endlessly.

The Bigger Picture

One party. One plan. One group chat. None of those defines your social future. Teen years can feel very immediate, like what happens this week determines everything. It doesn't. Friendships shift. Circles change. People mature. Your steadiness now matters more than one invitation.

Challenge Yourself: Try This

If you feel left out of something, instead of spiraling, do one small connecting action somewhere else. Text someone you trust. Start a new conversation with someone. Say yes to one different opportunity. Confidence grows when you move toward connection, not away from it.

Being left out hurts. But it does not get the final word on your value. And it certainly doesn't get to decide who you become.

When You Feel Left Out

Sofia learned about the party on Instagram. She wasn't invited. She didn't even know it was happening until she saw the photos, a group of girls from school smiling in someone's living room, holding red plastic cups filled with soda, laughing like they'd been planning it for weeks. Sofia stared at the pictures longer than she meant to.

Why didn't they invite me?
Did I do something?
Do they even like me?
Was everyone invited except me?

Her chest felt tight. Not angry exactly. Not even surprised. Just... small. If you've ever found out about something you weren't included in, you know that feeling. It's not loud like embarrassment. It's quieter. But it can hurt more.

Being Left Out Hits Deep

Here's something important to understand. Belonging matters. Humans are wired for connection. When we feel excluded, even in small ways, our brains react strongly. That doesn't make you dramatic. It makes you human. The problem isn't that it hurts. The problem is the story your brain may attach to the hurt.

The Stories We Tell Ourselves

When you feel left out, your mind may jump to conclusions like:

"They don't like me."
"I'm not important."
"I'm always the extra friend."
"I'll never fit in."

Those thoughts feel true in the moment. But they are interpretations, not confirmed facts. Let's slow it down. What are the actual possibilities?

- It was a smaller gathering.
- They invited people they sit with every day.
- Someone else organized it.
- It wasn't meant to exclude you personally.
- They assumed you were busy.

Are all of those guaranteed? No. But neither is the worst-case version. When something hurts, your brain looks for a clear explanation. It often chooses the harshest one.

Not Every Invitation Is a Measure of Your Worth

This is a difficult but freeing truth. You will not be included in everything. No one is. Even socially confident girls experience moments of exclusion. The difference is how they interpret it.

Instead of deciding: "I wasn't invited because I'm not good enough."

They think: "That event happened. I wasn't part of it. That doesn't define me."

That's steadiness.

Group Dynamics Are Complicated

Friend groups are rarely as simple as they look in photos.

There are:

- Sub-groups within groups
- People who are closer to some than others
- Situations that grow out of shared classes or activities
- Plans made quickly without deep thought

Sometimes you're not included because of proximity, not because you're rejected. It doesn't mean you don't matter. It means social circles are fluid. And fluid doesn't mean permanent.

What Not to Do When You Feel Left Out

When exclusion stings, your brain may suggest:

- Posting something to make them notice you
- Sending a dramatic text
- Pulling away completely
- Deciding you'll never try again

Those reactions feel powerful in the moment. But they rarely create the outcome you want. Instead, aim for calm. Not pretending it doesn't hurt. Just not letting the hurt control your next move.

A Steady Response

If you find out about something you weren't invited to, try this:

Feel it, without judging yourself for feeling it. Separate the event from the story. Stay consistent in your normal interactions. You don't need to act colder. You don't need to overcompensate. You don't need to prove anything. Steady confidence often looks quiet.

When It Keeps Happening

If you consistently feel left out around the same group, that's information. Not about your worth. About your fit in that particular group. Sometimes the healthiest move isn't forcing your way into a circle. It's expanding your circle.

That might mean: talking more with someone in a different class, joining a new club or activity, or strengthening one-on-one friendships. Belonging grows where effort is mutual. You don't have to chase it endlessly.

The Bigger Picture

One party. One plan. One group chat. None of those define your social future. Teen years can feel very immediate, like what happens this week determines everything. It doesn't. Friendships shift. Circles change. People mature. Your steadiness now matters more than one invitation.

Challenge Yourself: Try This

If you feel left out of something: Instead of spiraling, do one small connecting action somewhere else. Text someone you trust. Start a new conversation with someone. Say yes to one different opportunity. Confidence grows when you move toward connection, not away from it.

Being left out hurts. But it does not get the final word on your value. And it certainly doesn't get to decide who you become.

Understanding Rejection and What It Really Means

Emma had been building up courage for two weeks.

There was a boy in her history class who always made sarcastic comments under his breath, and they made her laugh. They talked a few times. Nothing serious. Just small conversations before class. Finally, she decided to try something small.

“Hey,” she said one afternoon, trying to sound casual. “A few of us are going to the game on Friday. You should come.”

He hesitated. “Oh. I already have plans.”

It wasn’t rude. It wasn’t dramatic. It was just... not what she hoped. Emma smiled and nodded like it didn’t matter. But later that night, it mattered a lot.

He didn't want to go. He was just being polite before. Why would I think he'd want to come?

Rejection doesn't have to be loud to hurt. Sometimes it's quiet. And that quiet can echo.

Why Rejection Feels So Personal

Rejection hits differently than awkwardness. Awkward moments are uncomfortable. Rejection feels like a verdict.

Your brain may translate it into something bigger:

"I'm not interesting." "I'm not enough." "I shouldn't have tried."

But let's slow that down. One person declining an invitation is not a verdict on your worth. It's a response to a situation. That's it.

The Difference Between "No" and "Never"

When someone says no to an invitation, to hanging out, to building something closer, your brain may quietly add the word *never*.

"He doesn't want to come" becomes "He will never want to hang out with me."

"She doesn't text back much" becomes "She doesn't like me at all."

But most social moments are about timing, mood, interest level, or circumstances. They are not permanent judgments. A no in one moment does not define every future possibility. And even if it does? That still doesn't define you.

Rejection Is Information, Not Identity

This is an important shift. Rejection gives you information.

It tells you:

• This person may not be interested. • This plan didn't line up. • This connection might not grow.

What it does not tell you is:

• You are unworthy. • You are unlovable. • You should stop trying forever.

Those conclusions come from fear, not facts.

Compatibility Matters More Than Popularity

Not everyone will connect with you. And you will not connect deeply with everyone. That's not failure. That's compatibility. Some people are drawn to loud energy. Some prefer quiet steadiness. Some bond over sports. Some over books. Some over sarcasm or sincerity. If someone doesn't move toward you, it may simply mean you're not a close match. And that's okay. You don't need to shrink or reshape yourself to be everyone's preference.

The Brave Part You Might Miss

When rejection happens, your brain focuses on the outcome. But pause for a moment. Look at what you did. You tried. You spoke up. You invited. You risked something. That takes courage. And courage builds your confidence, even if the answer wasn't what you hoped. The goal isn't to avoid rejection forever. The goal is to survive without losing yourself.

What Not to Do After Rejection

After a rejection, your brain may suggest:

• "Don't try again." • "Act like you don't care." • "Avoid them completely." • "Prove yourself somehow."

None of those reactions builds confidence. They build protection. Protection feels safe in the short term. But growth requires steadiness.

A Calm Recovery Plan

If someone declines an invitation or doesn't respond with interest, try this:

Keep your response simple and respectful. "No worries!" or "That's okay!" Don't over-explain. You don't need to justify yourself. Continue interacting normally later. Not colder. Not extra enthusiastic. Just steady. This sends a powerful message to them and to yourself. "I can handle this." And that confidence is attractive in friendships and dating alike.

When Rejection Actually Protects You

Here's something surprising: Sometimes rejection protects you. If someone consistently doesn't show interest, effort, or kindness, that's valuable information. It saves you from investing energy in a connection that wouldn't be mutual. Confidence isn't about convincing people to choose you. It's about recognizing when someone isn't choosing you and still staying grounded.

Try Something New This Week

If you experience rejection, big or small, remind yourself of two things: This is information, not identity. I can survive this without shrinking.

Then do one brave thing within the next week. Text someone else. Join a different group. Start another conversation. Not because you need to prove something. But because you refuse to let one "no" decide your future. Rejection hurts. But it does not get to define you. And it certainly does not limit who you become.

Recovering from Embarrassment

HANNAH DIDN'T MEAN TO say it that way.

They were all sitting in a circle during youth group, talking about weekend plans. Someone mentioned a new restaurant opening downtown.

Hannah jumped in. "Oh yeah, I heard that place is super expensive. My mom said it's overrated."

Silence. The girl whose family owned the restaurant was sitting two seats away.

Hannah felt the realization hit her like a wave. Her face got hot. Her stomach dropped. She tried to laugh it off. "I mean... that's just what I heard." The conversation moved on. But Hannah didn't.

All night, her brain replayed it.

Why would I say that? That was so rude. She probably hates me now. Everyone probably thinks I'm awful.

If you've ever said something wrong, tripped over your words, laughed at the wrong moment, or realized too late that you misunderstood something, you know this feeling. Embarrassment can feel enormous. But here's the truth: Embarrassment is uncomfortable. It is not permanent.

Why Embarrassment Feels So Intense

Embarrassment is your brain's alarm system for social mistakes. It says: "Something might have gone wrong. Fix it." The problem is that your brain doesn't always accurately assess the situation. It treats small missteps like social disasters. Your face heats up. Your heart speeds up. Your thoughts race. But most embarrassing moments are smaller than they feel. Much smaller.

The Replay Loop

After something embarrassing, your mind may replay it over and over. You hear your own voice. You picture people's faces. You imagine what they must be thinking. Here's what most teens don't realize: Other people usually stop thinking about your mistake long before you do. They move on. They get distracted. They think about themselves. But you're still replaying the moment like it's a movie that won't stop. That replay loop is optional. You don't have to keep pressing play.

The 24-Hour Rule

Here's a simple recovery tool: Give yourself 24 hours. That's it. If the moment truly needs repair, an apology, or a clarification, you'll still be able to handle it tomorrow. But don't assume you need to fix it immediately. Strong social confidence isn't rushing to erase every small mistake. It's staying steady long enough to see whether the mistake even mattered. Most of the time? It didn't.

When an Apology Is Helpful

Sometimes you do realize, calmly, that something needs to be addressed.

In Hannah's case, she might say the next day, "Hey, I realized what I said about the restaurant probably came out wrong. I didn't mean anything negative about your family." Simple. Clear. Calm. No dramatic over-explaining. No emotional collapse. Just steady correction. Most people respect that. And then they move on.

When It Doesn't Need Repair

Sometimes embarrassment is just... awkward timing. You laughed too loudly. You mispronounced something. You answered a question incorrectly. Not every uncomfortable moment requires a formal response. Sometimes the most confident move is to continue as normal. Confidence isn't acting as if nothing happened. It's acting like it wasn't the end of the world.

You Are Allowed to Be Human

Perfection is not a social requirement. In fact, trying to appear perfect often creates more tension than being real. People feel more comfortable around someone who admits small mistakes, laughs gently at herself, corrects calmly, and moves forward. Embarrassment doesn't erase your strengths. It proves you're participating. You cannot build friendships while staying invisible. And sometimes participation includes imperfection.

What Embarrassment Teaches You

Embarrassment isn't only discomfort. It's data.

It teaches you:

• To pause before speaking • To read the room • To clarify gently • To grow socially

That's development. Not failure.

Try to Remember This Week

The next time something embarrassing happens: Pause before spiraling. Ask: "Will this matter in a week?" If needed, offer a calm correction. Then let it go. Not because it didn't feel uncomfortable. But because you refuse to let one moment define you. Embarrassment fades. Growth stays. And confidence grows strongest in the moments when you stay steady after a mistake, not when you avoid mistakes entirely.

Joining Group Conversations Without Forcing It

Olivia stood just outside the circle.

Four girls from her math class were gathered near the bleachers before practice, talking and laughing. She recognized the topic, a substitute teacher who had mispronounced someone's name. She wanted to join. But she didn't want to interrupt. She stepped closer. Then stopped. Then pretended to check her phone. *Do I walk in? Do I wait for a pause? What if I say something weird?* She stayed quiet long enough that it felt even more awkward.

If you've ever hovered near a group conversation, unsure how to enter without making it strange, you're not alone. Group dynamics can feel intimidating. But they're not mysterious. They have timing.

Why Group Conversations Feel Harder

One-on-one conversations are simpler. You speak. They respond. Group conversations are different.

There are:

• Multiple voices • Shared history • Fast topic changes • Inside jokes

It can feel like jumping onto a moving train. The key is not forcing the jump. It's matching the speed.

Step One: Listen Before You Enter

Instead of speaking immediately, listen for a moment. What's the topic? Is it light or serious? Are they telling a story or debating something? Listening gives you context. And context makes your entry smoother. You don't need a dramatic introduction. You need alignment.

Step Two: Enter With Relevance

The easiest way to join a group conversation is to add something connected to what's already being said.

If they're talking about the substitute teacher, you might say, "He said my name wrong, too. I didn't even correct him." Or "Wait, was that the class where he mixed up the seating chart?"

Short. Relevant. Natural. You don't need to redirect the topic to something entirely new. That's when it can feel forced.

Step Three: Keep It Light at First

When joining a group, think small at first. One comment. One reaction. One shared laugh. You don't need to dominate the conversation. You're simply entering it. Confidence doesn't mean taking over. It means participating calmly.

If No One Responds Immediately

Here's an important truth: Sometimes you'll add something, and it won't get much of a reaction. That doesn't automatically mean you failed. In groups, conversations overlap. People talk over each other, timing shifts.

If your comment doesn't land strongly, don't panic. Don't over-explain. Don't withdraw dramatically. Stay present. You can try again naturally later. One quiet moment does not cancel your place in the group.

Body Language Matters More Than You Think

You don't have to say much to signal belonging. Stand open, not closed off. Make eye contact occasionally. Nod when someone speaks. Nonverbal cues communicate: "I'm part of this." And often, once you appear comfortable, others feel more comfortable including you.

When It's Not the Right Moment

There will be times when a group is deep in a private story or intense discussion. If the energy feels closed, meaning they're tightly focused inward, it's okay to wait. Waiting is not a weakness; it's awareness. You can always reconsider joining later in a different setting. Not every group moment is meant for entry. And that's okay.

The Difference Between Forcing and Flowing

Forcing looks like:

• Interrupting loudly • Changing the subject abruptly • Talking too long without feedback • Overcompensating with energy

Flowing looks like:

• Matching tone • Adding to the conversation briefly • Letting others respond • Staying steady

Confidence flows. It doesn't push.

The Quiet Confidence Advantage

Here's something powerful: The girl who enters a group calmly, listens well, and contributes thoughtfully often builds stronger long-term connections than the loudest voice in the circle. You don't need to be the most entertaining person in the group. You need to be present and consistent. Belonging grows from repeated small interactions. Not one big performance.

Try Challenging Yourself This Week

Find one group conversation this week and practice entering gently. Listen first. Add one relevant comment. Stay steady, even if the reaction is neutral. You don't need to impress anyone. You're just practicing presence. Because joining isn't about being perfect, it's about being willing to step in, without forcing your way. And that's a skill you can build.

Handling Cliques, Drama, and Social Pressure

Kayla used to sit with the same group every day.

They laughed about the same teachers. Shared snacks. Talked about the same shows. But lately, something felt different. Inside jokes she didn't understand. Plans mentioned after they were already made. Glances exchanged that didn't include her. No one had said anything unkind. But the circle felt tighter. And she felt just outside of it. If you've ever sensed a shift in a friend group, not dramatic, just subtle, you know how confusing it can be. It's not loud like rejection. It's quiet. Unsteady. And it makes you question yourself.

What Cliques Really Are

A clique is simply a tight-knit group. That's it. Sometimes cliques are healthy, built on shared interests, trust, and time. Sometimes they become exclusive in ways that feel sharp or unkind. But here's something important to keep in mind. Not every tight group is intentionally trying to exclude you. Sometimes people grow closer because of shared activities. Shared classes. Shared time. That doesn't automatically mean you've done something wrong.

When the Energy Changes

Social groups shift. That's normal. Teen years are full of change: interests evolve, schedules shift, and personalities develop. If a group's energy feels different, ask yourself, has something specific happened? Or has the dynamic shifted? There's a difference between intentional exclusion and natural change. Your job is to observe before reacting.

The Trap of Trying to "Earn" Your Place

When you feel slightly outside a group, your brain may suggest:

• Be louder. • Be funnier. • Change your style. • Agree with everything.
• Try harder.

But chasing approval often creates more anxiety, not more belonging. Real belonging doesn't require performance. If you have to reshape yourself to stay in a circle constantly, that circle may not be steady enough for you.

Handling Subtle Drama

Drama doesn't always look dramatic.

Sometimes it's:

• Whispering • Screenshots shared privately • Shifting alliances • "She said" conversations

When drama starts circulating, the safest move is usually to keep a calm distance.

You don't need to:

• Pick sides immediately • Spread information • Defend yourself aggressively • Join in to protect your spot

Drama feeds on reaction. Steadiness weakens it.

Social Pressure and Identity

Cliques sometimes come with unspoken expectations. Dress this way. Like this music. Laugh at these jokes. Don't hang out with them. Pause for a moment. If belonging requires you to abandon your values or personality, that's not belonging. That's pressure. Healthy friendships let you be yourself. They don't require shrinking or reshaping.

When to Stay and When to Expand

Not every shifting group needs to be abandoned. Sometimes you can stay steady, contribute calmly, and allow the dynamic to settle. But if you consistently feel tense, guarded, unwanted, or smaller than yourself, that's information. Not about your worth. About your environment. Expanding your circle isn't failure. Its growth.

The Confidence of Not Chasing

There is something deeply powerful about not chasing attention, staying kind, showing up consistently, and refusing to compete for space. Quiet confidence often stands out more than loud effort. And people notice steadiness over time, even if they don't say it right away.

Try Challenging Yourself This Week

If you feel pressure within a group, notice where you feel tension. Ask yourself: "Am I acting like myself right now?" Make one choice this week that reflects your real values, even if it's small. That might mean:

• Not laughing at a joke that feels unkind • Talking to someone outside your usual circle • Staying neutral during gossip

Belonging should feel steady, not exhausting. The strongest friendships are built on authenticity, not pressure.

Repairing Awkward Moments and Misunderstandings

Brianna didn't realize how it sounded until later.

During lunch, a girl in her friend group mentioned she was nervous about trying out for student council. Without thinking, Brianna said, "I mean... It's kind of a popularity contest anyway." She meant it as a joke. But her friends' smiles faded. The table got quiet for half a second. The conversation moved on, but something felt off.

Later that afternoon, Brianna replayed it.

That sounded rude. Did she think I was making fun of her? Should I say something? Or just let it go?

If you've ever walked away from a conversation thinking, "*That didn't come out the way I meant it,*" you're not alone. Misunderstandings happen. What matters is what you do next.

Why Repair Matters

Friendships aren't built on never making mistakes. They're built on handling mistakes well. Small tensions left unaddressed can grow quietly. But small corrections can strengthen trust. Repair shows maturity. It says: "I care enough to clear this up." That builds more confidence than pretending nothing happened.

First: Pause Before Reacting

Not every awkward moment needs immediate action. Sometimes your brain exaggerates the tension. Before sending a long text or apologizing dramatically, ask: Did something clearly go wrong? Or does it just feel uncomfortable? Give yourself a little space. If the moment still feels unsettled after a few hours or the next day, that's usually your cue that you need to say something.

Keep Repair Simple

One common mistake teens make is over-explaining. Long messages. Paragraph apologies. Emotional spirals. Repair doesn't need to be dramatic. It needs to be clear.

For example:

"Hey, I realized my comment earlier might've sounded dismissive. I didn't mean it that way."

That's it. No emotional collapse. No begging for reassurance. Simple, calm, and direct.

When You're Misunderstood

Sometimes you didn't say anything wrong, but someone took it differently from how you intended. That happens.

Instead of getting defensive, try:

"Oh wow, that's not how I meant it. Thanks for telling me."

That response does three powerful things:

• It lowers tension. • It keeps your dignity. • It shows emotional maturity.

You don't have to prove your innocence. You clarify your intent.

When Someone Doesn't Respond Warmly After Repair

Here's something important:

You are responsible for offering repair. You are not responsible for controlling their reaction. If you stay calm and the other person remains distant for a while, that doesn't mean you've failed. It means they're processing. Give people room. Confidence includes allowing space.

The Difference Between Guilt and Growth

Guilt says: "I messed up. I'm terrible."

Growth says: "I said something imperfect. I'll adjust."

One shrinks you. One strengthens you. You are allowed to make mistakes. You are also capable of handling them well. That's maturity.

When It's Not Yours to Fix

Sometimes tension isn't caused by you at all.

Maybe someone is:

• Having a bad day • Feeling insecure • Misreading tone • Projecting their own stress

Not every social shift requires you to step in and repair it. If you haven't done anything clearly unkind, you don't need to assume responsibility. Confidence includes knowing when to act and when to stay steady.

The Calm Follow-Up Formula

If you need a simple repair structure, use this: Acknowledge the moment. Clarify your intent. Keep it short. Example: "Earlier, I made that comment about the student council. I hope it didn't come off negatively. I didn't mean it that way." Then let it breathe. Most people appreciate directness. And most small tensions dissolve faster than your brain predicts.

Try Something This Week

If you notice a moment that feels slightly off, instead of replaying it endlessly, ask yourself: Does this need repair? If yes, keep it simple. If not, practice letting it go. You don't need to be perfect to build strong friendships. You need to be willing to correct gently when needed.

Repairing a mistake doesn't weaken your confidence. It strengthens it.

STOPPING THE REPLAY LOOP

MADISON SHOULD HAVE BEEN asleep. Instead, she was staring at her ceiling.

The sleepover had ended hours ago. Nothing dramatic had happened. No fights. No awkward silence that lasted too long. But her brain refused to rest.

Why did I tell that story about my old school? Was that too much? Did they think I was bragging? I talked more than usual. Was that annoying?

She replayed the exact moment she laughed too loudly. Then, the moment someone didn't respond right away. Then, the moment she interrupted without meaning to. By midnight, her mind had turned a perfectly normal night into a social disaster analysis.

If you've ever replayed a conversation long after it ended, you know how exhausting it can be. Sometimes the conversation is over, but your mind isn't.

Why Your Mind Replays Social Moments

Your brain is designed to learn from experience. After a test, it reviews what you missed. After a game, it remembers what worked. After social interactions, it does the same thing. But sometimes, instead of reviewing calmly, it overanalyzes. It looks for mistakes. It searches for signs of rejection. It zooms in on tiny details and treats them like major problems. The replay loop isn't a weakness. It's an overactive evaluation. And it can be redirected.

The Problem With Endless Reviewing

There's a difference between reflecting and replaying.

Reflection sounds like: "That part felt awkward. Next time I'll pause before jumping in."

Replay sounds like: "I ruined it. I always ruin things. Why am I like this?"

One helps you grow. The other drains your confidence. If your thoughts help you adjust gently, that's reflection. If they're attacking your identity, that's a replay.

Most People Are Not Replaying You

Here's something that might surprise you:

While you're replaying your own words, the other girls are probably replaying theirs. Everyone is thinking about themselves more than they are thinking about you. That laugh you thought was too loud? They may not remember it at all. That comment you worried about? They may have been distracted when you said it. Your brain assumes a spotlight is on you. But most people are holding their own spotlight.

The Two-Question Reset

When you catch yourself replaying a social moment, pause and ask:

1. Is this thought helping me improve, or just making me feel worse?

2. Will this matter in a week?

If the answer to the second question is no, your brain may be exaggerating the importance. Not every small misstep deserves a midnight review session.

Set a Time Limit on Reflection

If something genuinely feels worth examining, give it five minutes. Yes, five. Think it through calmly. Ask yourself: Did I say something unkind? Do I need to repair anything? Is there one small adjustment I'd make next time? Then close the mental folder. Confidence grows when you decide not to revisit something over and over. You can learn without looping.

Replace Replay With Reassurance

Instead of:

"Why did I say that?"

Try: "I participated. That's brave."

Instead of: "I talked too much."

Try: "I contributed. That's allowed."

Steady reassurance interrupts spirals. Not fake positivity. Just balance.

When the Replay Is Really About Insecurity

Sometimes the replay loop isn't about the specific moment. It's about a deeper fear. *What if they don't like me? What if I'm too much? What if I'm not enough?* That fear existed before the sleepover. The event just triggered it. In those moments, remind yourself: One interaction does not define your entire social identity. Confidence isn't built on flawless nights. It's built on showing up consistently, even when you feel unsure.

Try Interrupting The Replay This Week

The next time your brain starts replaying a social moment, say either out loud or in your head: "I've reviewed this enough." Then redirect your focus to something grounding: Music. Reading. A shower. Sleep. You don't need to earn rest by analyzing yourself. You are allowed to close the day without solving every social detail. Overthinking feels productive. But steadiness is stronger. And the most confident girls aren't the ones who never overthink. They're the ones who decide when to stop.

Becoming the Kind of Friend People Trust

AVERY DIDN'T NOTICE IT at first.

But over time, people started choosing her. They sat next to her in class and asked her opinion. They confided in her. She wasn't the loudest in the group or the funniest. She wasn't the center of attention. She was steady. When someone shared something personal, she didn't repeat it. When drama started, she didn't add fuel. When plans changed, she didn't panic. She showed up the same way, consistently. And people trusted that. If you've ever wondered how some girls seem quietly solid in their friendships, this is usually why. Trust grows from steadiness.

Confidence Isn't Flashy

We often imagine confidence as bold, outgoing, and always talkative energy.

But social confidence also looks like:

• Listening fully • Keeping promises • Responding calmly • Not over-reacting • Staying kind under pressure

That kind of confidence builds long-term friendships. It doesn't chase attention. It earns respect.

The Power of Emotional Stability

When someone is going through something difficult, who do they talk to?

Usually, the girl who:

• Doesn't gossip • Doesn't mock • Doesn't exaggerate • Doesn't make everything about herself

Emotional stability feels safe, and safety builds trust. You don't need to have perfect advice; you need to be consistent

Small Behaviors That Build Trust

Trust isn't built in one dramatic moment.

It's built through small, repeated actions:

• Texting back when you say you will • Keeping private things private
• Being honest without being harsh • Showing up when you commit
• Apologizing calmly when needed

None of these behaviors is flashy, but they're powerful.

When You're Tempted to Compete

Friend groups sometimes bring quiet competition. Who's funnier? Who's closer to whom? Who gets invited first? Competing for a position often creates insecurity. Instead, focus on contribution. What kind of energy do you bring?

Are you:

• Supportive? • Reliable? • Calm? • Encouraging?

Contribution builds belonging more effectively than competition.

The Long Game of Friendship

Teen friendships can feel urgent. However, the strongest friendships grow over time. They develop through shared experiences, small conversations, and mutual trust. You don't have to win people over instantly. You build connections slowly. That's normal. And it's healthier than chasing quick validation.

When Someone Doesn't Trust You Yet

Trust takes time. If someone doesn't open up immediately, that's okay. You don't need to force closeness. You can stay steady. Consistency often speaks louder than intensity. The more you show up the same way, calm, respectful, reliable, the more others relax around you.

Becoming Someone You're Proud Of

Instead of asking: "Do they like me?" Try asking: "Do I like how I'm showing up?" That shift changes everything. When you're proud of how you handle awkwardness, rejection, drama, and repair, your confidence becomes internal. And internal confidence lasts longer than social approval.

Try Something New This Week

Choose one small trust-building behavior to practice:

• Keep something private. • Follow through on a commitment. • Stay neutral during gossip. • Offer encouragement without expecting praise.

Confidence grows when your actions align with your values, not when you're constantly measuring how others respond. The most secure friendships aren't built on perfection. They're built on trust. And trust is built by girls who stay steady, even when social situations feel uncertain.

Social Confidence Is Built in Real Life

Ella used to think confident girls were different.

She imagined they never felt awkward. Never replayed conversations. Never got rejected. Never wondered if they were too much, or not enough. But over time, she noticed something else. The girls she admired most weren't perfect. They stumbled over words and had quiet days. They sometimes weren't invited. The difference wasn't that they avoided uncomfortable moments. It was that they kept showing up anyway. Social confidence isn't something you wake up with. It's something you build.

Confidence Isn't a Personality Type

You don't have to be loud. You don't have to be the funniest. You don't have to be the center of attention. Confidence isn't about volume. It's about steadiness. It's the choice to try again after a flat conversation.

It's staying calm after a short text response. It's surviving embarrassment without shrinking. It's handling rejection without losing your sense of worth. That's confidence. And you build it in real moments. Not in theory.

Every Chapter Was About Practice

When we talked about:

Awkward silences, you practiced staying steady.

Flat responses, you practiced not mind-reading.

Feeling left out, you practiced separating the event from the story.

Rejection, you practiced choosing growth over identity collapse.

Embarrassment, you practiced recovery instead of replay.

Group conversations, you practiced entering without forcing.

Drama and pressure, you practiced authenticity.

Repair, you practiced maturity.

Overthinking, you practiced stopping the spiral.

Trust, you practiced consistency.

None of these skills are built in one day. They're built in repetition. And repetition happens in real life.

You Will Still Have Hard Moments

Let's be honest. You will still have awkward conversations. You will still misread situations sometimes. You may still feel left out. Confidence doesn't remove discomfort. It changes how you respond to it. Instead of spiraling, you steady yourself. Instead of shrinking, you stay present. Instead of chasing approval, you choose authenticity. That shift changes everything.

You Don't Need Everyone

Here's something freeing: You don't need everyone to like you. You need a few safe, steady connections. Quality over quantity. Depth over drama. Belonging over performance. And those connections grow when you stop trying to impress and start showing up consistently.

Moving Forward

As you go back into school hallways, group chats, sports practices, youth group circles, and everyday conversations, remember, you are allowed to participate imperfectly. You are allowed to grow and learn. You are allowed to be steady. Every awkward moment you survive strengthens you. Every recovery builds resilience. Every calm response increases your confidence. Not because everything goes smoothly. But because you stayed.

One Final Practice

This week, choose one moment to lean into, not away from. Join one conversation. Send one message. Offer one comment. Stay one minute longer. Not to prove yourself. Just to practice presence. Because social confidence is not built in isolation. It's built in real life. And you are more capable and worthy than you think.

Thank you for letting me share your journey to social confidence. If you learned something new or feel more confident socially, please share and leave me a review. Reviews help my books to be seen and shared with other young women like you.

My link is: https://www.amazon.com/dp/1971604100

Victoria

Further Reading & Resources

THE IDEAS IN THIS book are drawn from years of research in psychology, adolescent development, communication, resilience, and healthy relationships. If you would like to learn more, these books and resources are excellent places to start.

Recommended Books for Teens

Borba, Michele. *Thrivers: The Surprising Reasons Why Some Kids Struggle and Others Shine.* Avery, 2021.

Damour, Lisa. *Untangled: Guiding Teenage Girls Through the Seven Transitions into Adulthood.* Ballantine Books, 2016.

Damour, Lisa. *Under Pressure: Confronting the Epidemic of Stress and Anxiety in Girls.* Ballantine Books, 2019.

Nelsen, Jane. *Positive Discipline for Teenagers.* Harmony Books, 2012.

Sisson, Julia V. Taylor. *The Less-Than-Perfect Girl.* Free Spirit Publishing, 2006.

Thomas, Jillian. *The Self-Confidence Workbook for Teens.* Althea Press, 2019.

Communication, Social Skills, and Relationships

Carnegie, Dale. *How to Win Friends and Influence People.* Simon & Schuster.

Cloud, Henry, and John Townsend. *Boundaries.* Zondervan.

Goleman, Daniel. *Emotional Intelligence.* Bantam Books.

McKay, Matthew, Patrick Fanning, and Kim Paleg. *Self-Esteem: A Proven Program of Cognitive Techniques.* New Harbinger Publications.

Anxiety, Resilience, and Emotional Health

Burns, David D. *Feeling Good: The New Mood Therapy.* Harper.

Dweck, Carol S. *Mindset: The New Psychology of Success.* Ballantine Books.

Neff, Kristin. *Self-Compassion.* William Morrow.

Seligman, Martin E. P. *The Optimistic Child.* Houghton Mifflin Harcourt.

Helpful Organizations and Resources

American Academy of Pediatrics
www.healthychildren.org

The Jed Foundation
www.jedfoundation.org

Mental Health America
www.mhanational.org

National Institute of Mental Health
www.nimh.nih.gov

ABOUT THE AUTHOR

VICTORIA PENLEY IS PASSIONATE about helping teen girls build confidence, healthy relationships, emotional resilience, and a strong sense of self.

With a background in psychology and Christian counseling, she has spent more than twenty years working with youth, older adults, and other at-risk populations. Throughout her career, she has helped people navigate challenges related to self-esteem, relationships, communication, personal growth, and life's difficult transitions.

Having struggled with social anxiety herself as a teen, Victoria understands what it feels like to overthink conversations, worry about fitting in, and question your own worth. Her goal is to provide practical tools, encouragement, and real-world guidance that help girls build confidence, trust themselves, and develop healthy relationships.

She is the creator of the **Girl Empowered! Series**, a collection of books designed to help teen girls build confidence, strengthen relationships, make wise decisions, discover their purpose, and navigate life's challenges with courage and self-respect.

Victoria lives in Idaho with her family and a cast of opinionated animals who occasionally inspire her writing.

To learn more about Victoria's books and upcoming projects, visit her author page on Amazon.

www.ingramcontent.com/pod-product-compliance
Lightning Source LLC
LaVergne TN
LVHW010942110826
845149LV00013B/2720
* 9 7 8 1 9 7 1 6 0 4 1 0 7 *